TEACHING LIFE SKILLS THROUGH CHESS

A GUIDE FOR EDUCATORS AND COUNSELORS

FERNANDO MORENO

American Literary Press, Inc.
Five Star Special Edition
Baltimore, Maryland

Teaching Life Skills Through Chess

Copyright © 2002 Fernando Moreno

All rights reserved under International and
Pan-American copyright conventions.
No part of this book may be reproduced, stored in a retrieval system, or
transmitted in any form, electronic, mechanical, or other means, now known
or hereafter invented, without written permission of the publisher. Address
all inquiries to the publisher. Permission is granted to use pages entitled
"puzzles" for educational purposes in classroom or clinical settings. These
pages may be reproduced in their entirety for this use only.

Library of Congress
Cataloging in Publication Data
ISBN 1-56167-704-3

Library of Congress Card Catalog Number:
2001095306

Published by

American Literary Press, Inc.
Five Star Special Edition
8019 Belair Road, Suite 10
Baltimore, Maryland 21236

Manufactured in the United States of America

This Book is dedicated to my parents:
Maria de los Angeles Izquierdo Luque,
and Rafael Moreno Hernando
who always showed me the right path to follow.

Acknowledgments

This book would not be possible without the encouragement of my wife, Matilde, and the editing and advice of my good friend, Denise Peterson and David Mehler, Director of the U. S. Chess Center.

Also, I would like to mention many people who have supported my work during my career. Thanks to: Ricardo Galbis, Conchita Espino, Erasmo Garza, Marjorie Myers, Elena Izquierdo, Maria Malagon, and my mentor and dear friend Vilma Montiel.

Finally, I have to recognize and give thanks to all the students and teachers who participated in my programs for all their positive energy toward my model of using the game of chess in counseling.

Contents

	INTRODUCTION	**1**
I	**CHESS AS AN ANALOGY TO LIFE**	**7**
	Rationale for Using Chess in School Counseling	8
	Chess Among School Counselors	16
II	**HOW TO USE CHESS IN COUNSELING**	**23**
	Classroom Guidance Presentations	27
	Group Counseling Sessions	30
	Individual Counseling	35
III	**DIRECTORY OF CHESS POSITIONS TO BE USED IN COUNSELING**	**43**
	Conflict Resolution /Fights	45
	Finding Your Own Skills	47
	Stealing	49
	Making Wise Decisions	51
	Goal Setting	53
	Short And Long Term Goals	55
	Healthy Development	57
	Taking Risks	59
IV	**CHESS COUNSELING PROGRAMS**	**61**
	Chess For Success	63
	Description Of Student Population	64
	Teacher Evaluations	66
	Student Evaluations	71
	Resources About Chess	**75**
	References	**77**

Introduction

Chess is an ancient table game. Nobody knows for sure who invented it, yet there are many legends about its origin. One of these tells about two kings in India. The kings asked their wisest men to invent a game that would test the two of them in a non-violent com-petition. The two kings played chess instead of fighting a war to resolve their differences without anyone getting hurt. Perhaps that worthy goal can be analogized to situa-tions that arise in schools every day.

Historians have concluded that the oldest known form of chess is Chaturanga. The game is believed to have originated in India between 500 and 700 A.D. and was a favorite leisure activity of the ruling class. Chaturanga used six kinds of pieces that were based on the Indian Army. Variations of the game developed from the original, leading to the game of chess that is now played universally. From India, the game traveled all over the world. Harold James Murray discovered that the first master chess players were Arabs. Chess came to America for the first time with Christopher Columbus and his fellow navigators and sailors who played chess during their long journey.

> **"Chess is an international language."**
> **Emmanuel Lasker**

Introduction

Chess is a very old game that is played all over the world. It may be the only game played by the same rules in every country in the world. Every country in the world has chess players; every city in this country has chess clubs. No matter where you go, you can find someone who plays chess.

With the recent increase in diversity in our public schools, chess can be an ideal tool for teaching that although we come from various backgrounds and speak different languages, our minds can work in similar ways when trying to reach a goal. I have seen many students from different cultures and backgrounds who did not know how to speak fluent English start interacting with others through a game of chess. They gained an appreciation of each other while playing chess, a "language" they had in common. The rules of chess are simple, but success in the game requires acknowledging your opponent's moves and planning your own strategy. Chess can be a bridge among different cultures.

As Benjamin Franklin noted many years ago, the value of learning and practicing the game goes beyond the recreational realm. While the skills learned in chess benefit everyone, chess has been known to be especially effective for students whose environments provide little or no resources for success in school or in society.

> " Chess is not merely an idle amusement...
> life is a kind of chess."
> Benjamin Franklin

Teaching Life Skills Through Chess

This book will describe how chess has helped thousands of students like the Royal Knights from East Harlem to become better students. Gloria Steinem told their story in the #1 New York Times Bestseller motivational book, *Chicken Soup for the Soul, 101 Stories To Open The Heart And Rekindle The Spirit.*

Bill Hall, an English and ESL teacher, works at Junior High School 99. His students arrived directly from South and Central America, the Caribbean, Asia, and Africa. These kids were faced with a new culture, strange rules, a difficult neighborhood and parents who were lost in the new culture. Bill, a chess player himself, knew that chess could cross the boundaries of culture. Bill introduced chess to them. It was not easy, but these kids improved in chess as well as in English. From Spanish Harlem they went to play successfully in the 1987 National Junior High School Chess Tournament. Later, the Royal Knights became the first American scholastic chess team to fly to the former Soviet Union to play chess. Chess taught them that they could do anything.

> **"Chess, like love, like music, has the power to make us happy."**
> **Dr. Siegbert Tarrasch**

The impact of chess in helping many students better understand the decision-making process and strategies for coping with problems and challenges has been widely documented.

Introduction

Perhaps not as documented is the change in perception teachers have when they find out their "problem students" are chess players. After counseling Jose, a 3rd grade Hispanic student for lacking motivation and achievement, his teacher told me: *"Jose has changed, he is more responsible with his things. He is doing his homework, but he is asking me to have a chess set in the class-room. That kid, he doesn't know how to play. Chess is very difficult. He can't do it. What have you done with him?"* I explained to her that I had taught him to play chess. I went on to explain that he was smart and could teach chess to anybody in the class, which was why he was asking for a chess set. Thereafter, the teacher expected more from that student, and he responded in a positive way. Chess helped him gain confidence and helped the teacher reach the conclusion that he was a bright student.

As mentioned earlier, the benefits of chess in the classroom appear frequently in the media across the U.S. Many television shows have documented educators who are using chess to help their students. Newspapers from California, Florida, Chicago, Boston, Washington, D.C., and many other cities have featured articles on the personal stories of kids whose lives changed because they were introduced to the royal game.

The primary focus of "Chess in Education" is the integration of chess into the school curriculum and into the teaching strategies employed during classroom time.

It does not exclude extracurricular chess clubs or scholastic tournaments, but the central point must be teaching chess to help students improve academic and social competencies.

The result of twenty years of educational research has been irrefutable. The Research Summary presented at the "Chess In Education: A Wise Move" conference in 1995 by Dr. Robert Ferguson has concluded that chess is an effective means of teaching critical thinking skills. Children who learn chess improve their performance in math and language arts. Many kids who have participated in chess programs have shown improvement in such social skills as responsibility, discipline, concentration and self-esteem as well as their academic performance.

> **"Children who learn chess improve their performance in math and language arts."**
> **Robert Ferguson, Ph.D.**

Chess enhances basic cognitive skills such as evaluating alternatives, scanning possibilities and options, decision-making, conditional thinking, planning short and long-term goals, following rules, and respecting others. Studies by Dianne Horgan, Ph.D., have concluded that chess will help students cope with the problems they will face in the academic and social worlds.

Chess also helps students learn such behaviors as waiting for one's turn, fair play and sportsmanship, losing graciously and showing respect when winning; practice and study are key for success, trying one's best, taking

Introduction

risks and assuming the consequences of one's actions, and above all having fun.

The U.S. Chess Federation (USCF) has a Chess in Education Committee which has presented seminars in conferences in many states. These seminars are designed to promote chess among schools and help educators to integrate chess into their daily teaching. For more information about how to integrate chess in the curriculum, contact Javier Pinedo, the Chair Person of the Chess in Education Committee.

The focus of this book is to help children develop social and cognitive skills rather than to create chess masters. Those children who do develop a great interest in the game of chess can find scholastic chess clubs in most cities. For information on local chess clubs contact the Scholastic Director of the U.S. Chess Federation. Also, the USCF office has materials on "How to Integrate Chess In The Curriculum" (Javier Pinedo, 1997) and "How to Best Teach Chess to Students" (Sunil Weeramantry, 1997).

Teaching Life Skills Through Chess

Chess As An Analogy To Life

Chess is played by two players on a 64-square board. Each player has 16 men. The players take turns moving one man at a time. The purpose of the game is to checkmate the king. A player must find a balance between protecting his or her king's safety and attacking the opponent's king.

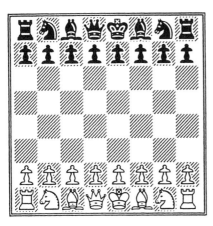

♔ 1 King

♕ 1 Queen

♖ 2 Rooks

♗ 2 Bishops

♘ 2 Knights

♙ 8 Pawns

Chess As An Analogy To Life

In this model of counseling, the chess board represents our lives.

> **Chess pieces are used as a metaphor for life situations.**

The board and pieces become a metaphor for our situation in life. The pieces become our skills and resources. The way we move them will lead us to success or failure. The other player represents the environment in which we live. We have control of our pieces, but we do not have control of how the other player moves. If we do not play with caution, we will be in danger of losing pieces and the game. This counseling model will teach children that they can take control of their own destiny by moving their "men" the right way.

Rationale For Using Chess In School Counseling

Educators and school counselors face the challenge of improving the academic and social-emotional achievement of students in public schools. Reports about the lack of student achievement and social skills are common headlines in newspapers, radio shows, and TV news. Former President Clinton initiated a movement to increase expectations and create national standards for reading skills in our schools (*The Washington Post, 1998*).

Teaching Life Skills Through Chess

Politicians across the states are thinking about cutting school counselor positions in order to put more reading teachers in our schools (*Counseling Today*, 1998). One of the greatest challenges for any school counselor is finding ways to address both the academic and social-emotional issues that prevent students from reaching their full potential. Teachers, parents and administrators need to see that their students are not just "wasting their time" talking about feelings in school. They must see that school counselors are using strategies that focus on students' academic achievement and success.

Because of all of these social pressures, school counselors cannot afford to focus exclusively on students' emotional needs. School counselors' work must be tied to academic achievement. Chess is the perfect tool for addressing this multifaceted challenge. As was mentioned in the Introduction, researchers have found the benefits of chess in the classroom. Several studies are noted for their amazing results among students exposed to chess. "The Effects of Chess on Reading Scores: District Nine Chess Program Second Year Report," by Dr. Stuart Margulies, is one such report in which students in a New York City Chess Program improved reading scores more than a control group.

With the academic and social development needs of students in mind, I developed a guidance and counseling model that incorporates both areas. This is how **Counseling Through Chess As An Analogy To Life** was developed.

For the past eleven years, I have been developing and using this model. It was first used in the District of Columbia Public Schools with students from Lincoln Middle School, Deal Junior High School, Tubman Elementary School, Bell Multicultural High School, and Bancroft Elementary School. During the past seven years, I implemented a counseling program called Chess for Success in Montgomery County Public Schools in Maryland.

This counseling model links chess strategies to guidance and counseling objectives. Beyond teaching the game of chess, it is a tool to help students explore the decision-making process, evaluate situations, and take responsibility for their actions. The program focuses on the development and reinforcement of social skills such as coping with feelings of frustration and anger, conflict resolution, self-control, self-confidence, self-respect, and understanding the process of goal-setting, success and achievement.

> **This model links chess strategies to guidance and counseling objectives.**

The general conceptual framework of this model is based in cognitive behavioral theory. The ideas in this manual are based on the premise that learning social skills is the foundation for social and academic capacity. By learning the game of chess as a metaphor for life and correlating the skills needed to play good chess with the skills needed in life, we accomplish our objective of addressing both academic and social-emotional skills.

The importance of social-emotional skills is well documented in the literature (Karin, F., 1999). Many researchers have demonstrated the benefits of social-emotional learning programs that work to foster empathy, emotional-regulation, problem solving, and impulse control skills (Gottma, Katz & Hooven, 1997).

Daniel Goleman, in his book *Emotional Intelligence* (1995), writes about the social skills that a person needs to have to succeed in today's society. It is not only our pure intelligence that helps us to achieve, it is also our social emotional competence. Many of the social skills we need to be successful in life can be learned by playing chess and seeing it as a metaphor for life.

Ferran Garcia Garrido, (2001) in his Book *"Educando desde el Ajedrez"* favorably describes programs that link chess in the classroom. He also enumerates emotional skills that are linked to chess.

The next table compares some of the skills (left side) that the W.T. Grant Consortium (David Hawkins et al.,1992) concluded are key factors of effective programs to promote social competence with the skills that chess develops.

Skills Table

SKILLS YOU NEED IN LIFE	SKILLS THAT CHESS DEVELOPS
Emotional Skills	
• Managing feelings	• You need to manage feelings in every position of the game.
• Controlling impulses	• If you do not control your impulses, you might move too fast and not see that your chess piece or position is in danger.
• Delaying gratification	• Sometimes in a chess position it is better not to capture a piece.
• Identifying and labeling feelings • Expressing feelings • Assessing the intensity of feelings • Knowing the difference between feelings and actions	• Playing chess offers an opportunity to discuss feelings that arise in different situations. For example: "I made a mistake..., I hope he does not see it..., I'm afraid of losing that piece...".

Teaching Life Skills Through Chess

• *Reducing stress*	• One skill necessary to perform well in school and in chess is to control and reduce stress when taking a test or playing a match. In counseling sessions, I explain what stress is and how to cope with it. Chess matches can be very stressful, but we need to learn to deal with that stress to make the most of our opportunities.
<u>*Cognitive Skills*</u>	
• *Self-talk: conducting an "inner dialogue" as a way to cope with a topic or challenge or reinforce one's own behavior*	• To understand a chess position you have to "self-talk" it. For example, you say to yourself: "…What pieces are attacking my pieces…"
• *Using steps for problem solving and decision making, for instance, controlling impulses, setting goals, identifying alternative actions,*	• When you play chess you have to make decisions and resolve situations every time you move a piece. You must control your impulses; because if you move too

anticipating consequences.	quickly, one of your pieces can be captured. You must set short and long-term goals to achieve a better position and win the game.
• *Understanding the perspective of others*	• To play chess, you must try to understand what the other player is planning. It is not unusual in high-level play to see players get up and look at the board from the other side.
• *Understanding behavioral norms (what is and is not acceptable behavior)*	• In chess, you must follow behavioral as well as the basic rules of etiquette.
• *A positive attitude toward life*	• In chess, you try to find the best choice in each position. If you think that you are in a very weak position, you must learn from it to gain insight for future games.
• *Self-awareness, for example, developing realistic expectations about oneself*	• In chess, you learn that other players are better than you and that you are better than others.

Teaching Life Skills Through Chess

Behavioral Skills	
• *Nonverbal communicating through eye contact, facial expressiveness, tone of voice, gestures, and so on*	• In chess you learn to see non-verbal clues from your opponent.
• *Verbal: making requests clearly, responding effectively to criticism, resisting negative influences, listening to others, helping others, participating in positive peer groups*	• When you are conducting a chess class, you point out mistakes players made. Sometimes they play on a team (4 against 4). They need to learn and cope with negative influences from their team. They are recommended a move that you know is not good. You also need to learn how to listen to other points of view in order for your team to win. Chess is a positive and healthy activity that kids enjoy very much.

This table above shows the clear parallel between the emotional skills we need to develop to become successful and happy members of society with the skills developed in learning the game of chess.

Chess As An Analogy To Life

Chess Among School Counselors

School counselors are one of the most important agents in education. I had the opportunity, thanks to the sponsorship of the U. S. Chess Federation, to have an exhibit about chess at the National Conference of the School Counselors Association held in San Antonio, Texas, in 1998. More than 300 school counselors from around the country had the opportunity to be introduced to the chess materials displayed at this booth.

Many counselors who passed by the booth asked me the question, "Why are you here?" The response was easy for me. Any educator who had already used chess did not have any reservation about its value and success. But for many counselors, it was the first time they dared to see this game in a different way. I distributed literature and research papers to show the benefits of chess and how I was using it in counseling.

After I explained how learning to play chess and participating in chess related activities could help students improve their achievement and social adjustment in school, the counselors understood why we were there. However, some counselors were not an easy audience, several counselors said something like: *"Chess, No!, this is not for me."* It took some effort to persuade them to listen to and look at the materials. But after engaging them and showing pictures, literature and explaining how this model works, almost all of them started to warm up to the idea.

Teaching Life Skills Through Chess

The most difficult task I encountered was convincing them that learning the "Counseling Through Chess As An Analogy To Life Model" is like learning any other counseling model. Many counselors worry when they see the word, "chess". They are afraid they cannot use and learn this approach.

One of the first reasons not to pay attention to this approach initially is that they themselves have not been exposed to the chess game and its values. In this country, chess is perceived as a "man's" game and many women were not encouraged to learn this game. A large percentage of school counselors in the U. S. are female. Anne, a counselor in San Antonio commented: *"I do not know how to play, so how can I benefit from learning about chess..."*. To this I replied, *"I am not an actor, but I can use role playing with my students. If you think that this model is beneficial, no matter how old you are, you will learn to play chess and to use it with your students"*.

Another reason for not pursuing the model is the perception that chess is very difficult to learn and you need to play very well in order to use it. Some counselors started changing their minds when they saw pictures of my first grade counseling groups playing chess. One elementary counselor commented," *I did not think that a first grade student could learn to play*".

The counselor does not need to be skilled in chess to use this model. Some of the students I help learned the game well enough to beat me. Learning chess has many levels like education. Just as you do not need to be a Ph.D. to teach a first grade student, you do not need to be a chess

Chess As An Analogy To Life

master to introduce the game, teach some basic lessons, and counsel students through chess. For counseling purposes you only need to learn how the pieces move, some simple chess tactics, some strategy and some basic checkmates. Remember that the objective in this model is establishing the counseling relationship and not creating chess masters. If a student becomes a great player and is interested in the game, you can find somebody from the community to help develop this talent in chess.

> **You do not need to know how to play very good chess to use this approach.**

Also, by trying to learn the game with your students, you will gain rapport and trust. When a counselor is learning the game, he or she feels insecure, confused, often not knowing what to do. This is how the students feel when they are in the counselor's office. The counselors' feelings are used to open up the rapport. You share those insecurities with the students. You might say *"I'm confused here... I don't know what to move next...., this happens to you, doesn't it?"*. Sometimes, your own difficulties are positive outcomes for your students. The students have the opportunity to gain insight because of your difficulties. They will see us as role models. Our own difficulties and struggles in learning the game along with the mistakes and frustration of losing will help them to understand and cope with their problems and difficulties.

Learning the basics of chess is not very difficult, if it is taught the right way. For example, you do not start teaching chess with all the pieces on the board. You start with only one piece at each time. For many of the counselors I spoke with, this was the first time they had heard about teaching chess. Angela, a counselor from Arizona, commented to me: *"When I was a little girl, I did not like it, because when my father tried to teach me, it was so confusing. It was so difficult to learn all the pieces and how each was moved."* She later said, *"But now that you have explained how to teach chess. I think I can learn it and my students can enjoy it too."*

There are many good books about teaching chess and the U. S. Chess Federation has many materials that can help anybody who is interested in learning more. The U.S. Chess Center, in Washington D. C. has developed a chess manual that is very easy and friendly to use.

As previously noted, there are several references in the literature about the value of chess in education. Also, there are many therapeutic board games that have been created for use with kids. However, there are few references, about the use of chess in counseling or therapy. The author's search of the professional literature has revealed very little on this subject.

In the book, called *Elementary School Counseling in the New Millennium* edited by Daya Singh Sandhu (2001), Kelly Cooker wrote: "Playing board games can be a valuable tool for social learning"... "Simple games such as Chinese Checkers, Candyland are generally better to use than more complicated games such as Monopoly or Chess (Oaklander, 1988).

Chess As An Analogy To Life

The book called: *Game Play: Therapeutic Use of Childhood Games* (1986), has a reference about the use of chess. *"Complex strategy games however, such as chess or Stratego, are often time-consuming, intellectually draining affairs leaving little time or energy for therapeutic work."* Richard Garden (1986) wrote *"The game of chess, however, has lower psychotherapeutic value. Whereas a game of checkers can generally be completed within 10 to 15 minutes, the game of chess rarely can and usually goes beyond the standard 45 to 50 minute session. Continuing in the next session is impractical because the likelihood of all the pieces being in the same place at the time of the next session is extremely small."*

These references express the opinion that chess doesn't have much therapeutic value. Their perspective is based on the assumption that these games (structured) do not elicit fantasy and the therapist does not learn much about the unconscious processes.

Nevertheless, my experience has shown the great value of using chess with "at risk" students. As described in chapter four, students and teachers positively evaluated the program that I conducted using chess in counseling. They commented on the positive value which also contradicts these statements. Also, the author's consideration of chess in therapy was limited to teaching social skills such as fair play and turn-taking. In my experience, chess is an ideal tool for teaching more abstract social skills such as decision making, goal setting and the difference between long term and short term consequences. In addition, a chess game does not have to last 40 minutes. Many of the games I play with kids last 10 to 15 minutes. You can play with fewer pieces or play speed chess. Also, you do not need to finish the game. The process is more important than the result. Finally, you can stop a chess game, write the positions of the pieces down, and, if you want, continue playing the game later.

Furthermore, some school counselors are already reporting the use of chess. In a report by Christine Palm (1990), a guidance counselor, Jerome Fishman, from New York commented: *"Aside from being good for the cognitive development, chess develops their social skills too. I like the aspect of socialization. It helps kids learn how to be better friends"*.

Another counselor using chess as a counseling tool is Beulah McMeans in P.G County, Maryland. She teaches students that patience, self-discipline, and playing by the rules are part of the game (Leff,1993).

I had the opportunity to meet some counselors who were already using chess in their offices. Shanna Gilmer, from New York told me that she used chess at school. She shared that some teachers had criticized her because she was only playing games with students and not counseling them. She was very glad to see all the chess materials I presented to her and how beneficial they are for students. She told me that she will feel more confident when responding to any body who questions her about using chess as a tool to help students succeed in school. She also said, *"I'm glad that I'm not alone in using chess as a guidance, and counseling tool."*

The Today publication from the NEA featured an article in their Innovators section about this counseling model titled, "Chess for Success" in its January 1997 issue. The American Counselor Association publication, *Counseling Today* published an article in June of 1998. Peter Guerra called it "Counseling program uses chess as an analogy for life situations."

Many school counselors who read the articles, and/or attended any of my presentations in conferences commented positively about the approach. Some of them are starting to use chess in their work.

In September of 1996 at a reception at the U. S. Capitol Building, I received a National Award from the Chess in Education Committee from the USCF. The award read, *"Mr. Moreno developed the program to address the academic and social needs of all students. The USCF commends his initiative in employing chess strategy to teach real life lessons."*

I hope that this book will elicit more interest for counselors or any other mental health professionals to start using and/or researching the chess game in their work with young people.

How To Use Chess In Counseling

There are many books in counseling that describe in detail all the procedures and activities that a counselor must use to follow their model. This book is not written that way for a simple reason. I believe that each relationship established between a counselor and his or her student is unique and different. The same detailed procedures will not work with each student. Counselors learning the general idea and concepts from this model must elect the specific way they want to counsel their students. They must follow this model by using their counseling style and objectives and match them to the specific issues that the students are facing. We must focus on their individual needs and specific problems.

While this approach is primarily designed for school counselors to use, it can be easily adapted by any educator

How To use Chess In Counseling

and/or other mental health professional to conduct guidance and counseling sessions in their classroom and/or offices.

In this book, I describe general principles and counseling techniques that I have used, but the specific implementation depends on each of the counselors who use this model. Each counselor must decide how and when to incorporate this approach in their counseling sessions. Sometimes, I use it in coordination with role playing, or traditional play therapy where the chess pieces are the toys. The counselor must understand the relationship he wants to establish and choose the therapeutic moments in which to use this approach.

This approach serves as prevention for all children, as well as, intervention for "acting out" children. This model, like many others in counseling, does not work with all of our students' problems. But I personally have used chess with kindergarten through 12th grade students, including some in Special Education classes, Gifted and Talented classes and English as a Second Language classes with issues of:

- Families with alcohol or/and substance abuse

- Violence at home

- Lack of motivation/achievement

- Classroom discipline issues

- Adjustment/acculturation to a new country/school

- Separation from parents

- Fights. Conflicts with other students

- Lack of self-concept and self-esteem

- Lack of good decision-making skills such as:

    - High risk of pregnancy, SST and HIV

    - High risk of dropping out of school

    - High risk of involvement in alcohol/drugs substance abuse

It is very important when we are using this model not to lose the focus in the counseling relationship. The counselor must be prepared to avoid playing chess for his/her own amusement. Playing chess is fun, and if both the counselor and student are enjoying themselves it might improve the counseling relationship, but it is not the main purpose of the counseling session.

The counselor uses chess positions to mirror real life situations.

The counselor must focus on the individual counseling objectives and how his or her students gain insight about them during the game of chess. If the student likes to play chess more often, the counselor must provide an avenue for doing so. For example, counselors may help the school by creating a chess club after school or during recess where chess could be played at a competitive and recreational level. Many students who are referred to counselors will benefit by getting involved in an extra curricular activity such as chess. Also the chess club can be a follow-up tool for the counselor because of the high volume of students who have to be counseled in school.

In each game of chess, there are dozens of different positions with millions of potential combinations. Just as the chess positions are different, each student's problems are unique and different too. As counselors, we learn to recognize problems that are alike (the problems may be similar, but the circumstances and people are different) and create plans to help the students to cope with them. The same happens in a chess game. We learn to recognize positions and patterns of problems and how to resolve them. The student can gain insight by practicing different moves, just as in the counseling relationship when we ask students to practice different behaviors.

> **The creativity and experience of the counselor using this model is crucial.**

Sometimes when we ask a student to come to the counseling office, he or she is scared. Sometimes students do not like to talk. But when we tell them that we are going to play chess, the students feel less threatened and like it. This is very useful in the primary grades. During the game, the conversation starts and students open up and talk about their problems in relation with the chess position.

I will list general procedures for individual and small groups as well as guidance presentations. I will explain several chess positions that I use to initiate a discussion. Other times, when the students are playing with me and/or in groups, I stop the game to help them gain insight about a particular chess position as it relates to their personal issues.

The long term effectiveness of this approach and skills presented in this book requires applying the skills to real life situations.

Classroom Guidance Presentations

I developed a guidance lesson plan to be implemented in the classroom. It follows personal and social development and decision making as well as academic achievement competencies. It can be modified to fit the specific needs of each level. The times and days of implementation must be modified to match the specific needs of the audience.

Example of a Lesson Plan

Session	Social Development Objectives	Comments/ Tasks	Chess Objectives	Follow-up activities
1	To assess attitudes about school, self and others	It is important to follow rules.	* Introduction of the chess game and the rules * Board and pieces	* Name of the pieces. * Rank, file, diagonal.

How To use Chess In Counseling

Session	Social Development Objectives	Comments/ Tasks	Chess Objectives	Follow-up activities
2-3-4	To develop an appreciation of individual differences	-Each chess piece moves in a different way. -We are each different. -We have different strengths	*To learn how each piece moves: *Pawn *Bishop *Rook *Queen *King *Knight *castling	*Pawns vs. pawns *Bishops vs. Rooks *Queen vs. Pawns *Knights vs. Pawns *Queen vs. Rooks .
5	To develop respect for self and others	-How does my behavior affect others? -How do my own decisions affect my success in school, life, and the game?	* To learn that each move has a positive or negative consequence * To learn the rules of etiquette (shaking hands, touch move)	*Chess position Who will win? * Chess position Bishop vs. Pawns * Chess position Rooks vs. Pawns
6-7	To develop abilities and control emotions to make better decisions	Who is in control?	*To learn how to evaluate positions to make good decisions	* Chess position Conflict resolution * Chess position Who will win?

28

Teaching Life Skills Through Chess

Session	Social Development Objectives	Comments/ Tasks	Chess Objectives	Follow-up activities
8-9	To develop goal setting skills	What are your goals? Short and long term goals.	* Pawn promotion * Check * Checkmate * Stalemate	* Chess position Pawn promotion * Checkmate with Rooks * Checkmate with Queen * Stalemate position
10	To reinforce the importance of study skills	We learn by reviewing.	* To learn to write chess games	* Review games

Group Counseling Sessions

I start the group sessions explaining the purpose and goals of the group. I describe how we will use the game of chess as our tool to discuss and learn things. In group counseling sessions, I encourage more group discussion, than I would in classroom guidance presentations. We discuss the lesson as a whole group, after that, the group is divided in several subgroups of three or four players

How To use Chess In Counseling

who play each other. In the beginning the students play as a team. Two students facing two other students. In this way, each subgroup must help each other to find the best or correct move. I go around to each group observing how they play. I always reinforce with positive comments when I see that they are moving in the right way or they have planned a good strategy. It is important not to discourage students by making negative comments. All amateur players can always find better moves to do.

When I observe a chess position that may reflect a good example of a situation that the group or somebody in the group needs to face, I stop the game and we discuss it. *"Think before you move and evaluate the consequences of your moves. What is going to happen if you move that piece? What is your goal?"* are some examples of comments I have made to students. I have used concrete life situations that the students are facing or have faced in the past. After our discussion they resume playing their games.

In each subgroup I form, I try to balance chess levels. It is important to pair them by levels. Winners play winners and losers play losers. In this way, there will be few if any players who lose all the time. Also, I change teams so that weak players are paired with good players.

Many times I use some members of the group to teach other members. The activity of teaching a new student has helped many students with their self-confidence. Other times, I ask them to play with different groups of pieces.

Teaching Life Skills Through Chess

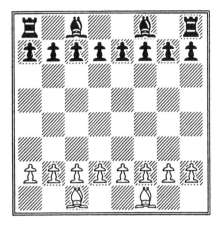

One group will have pawns, bishops and rooks and the other group will have only bishops. I will give students who lack self-confidence and hence have a greater need to win, the side with the greater force. I assign the less valuable pieces to the students who appear to have more confidence. The students who play with less valuable pieces sometimes argue that it is not fair to play that way. I explain that life many times is not fair, but each person has to make the best of each situation. Sometimes you are in a disadvantageous situation, but if you think and move in the right way, you will have success. You always have a chance to win in this game, as all it takes is one pawn reaching the other side of the board.

It is essential to explain to students when they are in the group that it is more important to learn the game than it is to win. It is natural for kids to like to win and want to finish their games, but sometimes I stop a game before it reaches the checkmate position. I point out to them the importance of their own improvement. We discuss how we feel during the game and how these feelings may affect our concentration and our decisions. Here, it is important to try to transfer the analysis of life situations and how our feelings affect our actions.

How To use Chess In Counseling

Sometimes I use big chess pieces, and we play on the floor. This has helped students to feel more comfortable because they can move around. With big pieces, I allocate four players to each team. They have to take turns because only one player from each team can move the piece. But other members of their team may suggest moves to make.

The counselor waits and observes the dynamics, and when the time is right; stops the game and discusses how peer pressure affects our decisions. For example, sometimes a bad move is suggested. If the person moving the piece follows a "bad" suggestion without giving it adequate thought, the team may lose a piece. There are bad consequences that follow from following somebody's suggestions without first thinking about it. Many times a student says to the other member of his team: *"It is your fault, you made me do it."* I say to them, *"No. You are responsible for your own actions."* We discuss how this relates to other things in their life like peer pressure to use cigarettes, drink alcohol or abuse other drugs, skip school, etc. We stop the game and focus on the skills we need to learn to avoid negative peer pressure.

Sometimes I make a very bad suggestion for a team to move a chess piece. If the team follows my bad advice, it loses a piece. When that happens, members of the team are very mad at me because I told them to make a foolish move. I stop the game and say, *"I know that you are mad because I suggested a bad move, but you should have recognized that this was a 'bad' move and not have made it. Sometimes older people can make suggestions to do things, but you have to be alert and decide if they are*

Teaching Life Skills Through Chess

good choices to follow. You do not need to make a move because I tell you to do it. You must decide before you act if it is good." I stop the game and resume the chess game position before my suggestion. Later in the game, I try to do it again. In almost all the groups, they do not accept my "bad suggestion." Each member helps each other in a "positive way" to see the better choice. I stop the game and say, *"You see, you can make good decisions, you can do the same in your life/school."*

This technique can be used to follow any other counseling objectives that the counselor is working on in the session. For example, in one of my groups there was a problem because a new student was being called names by another student. Some classmates were also calling her names because they said *"everybody is doing it."* We discussed this problem in the context of my "bad suggestion." I asked them if they knew it was wrong to call somebody names... I showed them how this was like moving the wrong chess piece at the suggestion of others.

Other counseling objectives I discussed in the groups include how each student is unique and how they have to develop, learn, and feel comfortable about who they are. The same happens when we study how the chess pieces move. Each chess piece is unique and moves in a different way. A knight moves in a different way from the bishop. But both of them are important. In some situations a knight can be more important than a bishop and vice versa. We must appreciate and learn the value of each piece in the same way we should appreciate and value the differences among us. In chess, you cannot only use one piece to win, you need to know and use all the pieces.

How To use Chess In Counseling

The same happens in our society. We must appreciate every person who is different or who is from another culture and learn from them.

When I talk with students who come from other cultures and countries with various languages, we discuss issues of acculturation, adjustment, and bilingualism and biculturalisim. I use this analogy with chess pieces. I ask them which is better: the Rook, the Bishop or the Queen. Many say the Queen. I tell them, "Yes, and the same thing applies to you."

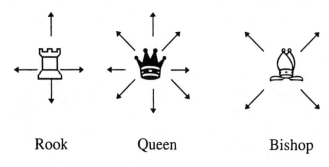

Rook   Queen   Bishop

I explain that rooks move horizontally and vertically; bishops move only diagonally, but the queen moves horizontally, vertically and diagonally. If you know one language it is good but, it is better if you can use two languages. The queen moves like a rook and bishop together. From here we discuss what it means to be bicultural and how it affects them.

It is important to focus our analysis on how the group discusses a chess position. We can observe the dynamics of students exhibiting a lack of acceptance of criticism, lack of listening skills, lack of attention…etc.

Sometimes, I start the session with a prepared position that reflects a specific student problem. The discussion that follows is directed to see the alternatives and to find better choices to resolve the situation. Because it is a chess position, students are encouraged to join the conversation and that makes it easier to get them involved with the discussion of the situation that we need to discuss. In the next chapter, I explain in detail some of the chess positions I use.

Individual Counseling

Chess is a perfect tool for establishing a quick and comfortable rapport with kids. Children generally like to play chess. I can spend several sessions only teaching pawns. The same is true with each of the other pieces. You do not need to teach the whole game immediately. With only a few pieces on the board you can start your counseling. After learning the moves, we focus on the specific problem that the student has and we relate the discussion toward that problem.

I tell the students: *"Your pieces are you and my pieces are the environment and the challenges you face. You have in your hands the way to cope and win if you make the right decisions."* From there, I start teaching, and we play chess.

Each piece can represent the skills a student needs. They must learn how each piece moves and the rest of the rules of chess just as they must learn academic and social skills

How To use Chess In Counseling

to live in our society. Students who are having difficulties following classroom rules might benefit from this exercise: When we are playing chess, I intentionally break a rule and change how a piece moves. Normally I capture their queen. The student says *"No, you cannot do that!"* I say: *"Why?"* Many times the students reply with something like: *"Because the rules say that you cannot move that way."* So at this point I confront them and say, *"But you are doing the same thing in the classroom, by doing ...(whatever infraction has been committed)."*

We discuss how by creating my own rules and not following the rules of the game, chess is not fun and we cannot learn much. I advise them that the same happens in the classroom. You must follow the rules to have fun and learn. I use this example of breaking the rules several times, until the student gets tired and a little upset. I say to him/her: *"This is the way your teacher feels sometimes when you are breaking all of the rules."*

Once, I received a referral for a student named Juan who had discipline problems and demonstrated a lack of motivation. He had been separated from his mother for more than five years. I used a behavioral contract using the chess pieces as incentive. Each time he lived up to the terms of the contract, he would win a chess piece. I asked the student to draw the chess pieces, and we gave the pictures to the teacher. When he finished all sixteen pieces, he was given a chess game. Like Juan, I had several first grade students who turned around their classroom behavior and homework assignments because of it.

Teaching Life Skills Through Chess

It is difficult to explain and help primary school students who come from alcohol and substance abuse families the concept of "locus of control." Many feel responsible for the situation and lack a sense of security. I use the analogy that in a chess game you have control only of your pieces and you do not have control over the other player's reactions. If you use your pieces well, have a goal and a purpose, and make wise decisions, you have a chance to win the game. The students need to know that while they do not have control over their parents' drinking habits, they still can help themselves do well in life.

Also, I use this model of control with kids who have issues of domestic violence, child abuse, etc.

When I counsel immigrant students who have come only recently to this country, I have to develop their motivation to learn from their first day of school. Many feel frustrated because of the difficulty of learning in a second language. Their self-esteem may be low when they do not understand some things in school. Some classmates laugh at them because they mispronounce English words. But people do not speak while playing chess. The faces of these newcomers reflect their growing confidence as they play with other kids in their classroom and beat them. This experience helps them to try harder in the academic realm.

I use chess with young people who have problems with self-control and impulsiveness, helping them to learn, practice, and see that each action has a consequence. In chess, when you move a piece, you cannot take back that move although you realize that it was a "bad" one. We discuss this lack of control and their impulsiveness in relation to actions that happen at school or at home. Many times, if you do not think, you can lose an important piece. Also, I help them to distinguish between their actions and themselves. These young people are generally criticized a lot for their lack of control. They hear many times "You are bad." We discuss that they are not bad, their actions (moves) are incorrect. Sometimes, after few sessions learning chess with me, I ask them to teach chess to other students. They start seeing themselves as a positive role model. They do not need to put down other kids or bully them. They can start feeling part of a group in a positive way by teaching others to play.

Sometimes, I use chess while counseling students from underprivileged backgrounds who are not motivated to learn. They have developed a sense of failure. Chess helps them learn that they can be successful in something if they work hard. I teach them step-by-step and help them feel they are improving. I use the analogy that each student is like a pawn. The pawn does not have the power or speed of a rook or queen. But it has the potential to reach the end of the board and change into any other piece. Just as the pawn may be promoted to any piece, the students can become anything they are willing to work towards.

I once counseled a student named Peter, who was living in a shelter. He had learned to play chess very well. I asked him to play using only his eight pawns against an inexperienced student who was given two rooks and eight pawns. The stronger player told me that such a start was unfair and that his opponent had such a large advantage that the outcome was predetermined. I told him that

Teaching Life Skills Through Chess

while perhaps the player with the superior forces had a greater likelihood of success, he would not have any chance of victory unless he tried to win. During the game he promoted one of his pawns to a queen and later captured his opponent's pieces and won the game. During the discussion that followed I congratulated both of them. To the student who lost, I explained that we need to use our abilities to their full potential; sometimes when we feel we are superior we do not try as hard and sometimes we lose when we should win.

For the student living in the shelter who won, we discussed that he needs to do the same in his life as he did in the game: work hard, make good choices, try his best and have a plan. By doing that he will be successful in life.

He must understand and cope with his family and life situation, but he must learn to use the resources he has available to him: his mind, school, teachers, friends, recreational facilities, and so on.

I use the game in which one of the players has fewer pieces with students who do not want to try because they feel they do not have any chance of being successful in school. I do not deny or minimize their difficulties. Rather, I challenge them to do better like in chess when they have less chances of winning. I explain that it is not easy because many times you don't win, but you try harder the next time.

I had another student named Abdul, ask me why the white pieces move first in a game of chess. Why can't the black pieces start first? I told him that this appears unfair, because white appears to have a little more advantage. I analyzed this comment and discussed it in the context of the racial situation in the U.S. Although there has been much progress to equal the opportunities in this country, if you are white you have more chances to succeed, as you do not face the barriers of racism. But the challenge that I put back to this African-American student was: *"Unfortunately the rules of chess say that white goes first. Until the rules change, what are you going to do.? Are you going to try harder to win with the black pieces or are you not going to try harder because it is unfair?."* As I point out to the students, the grand master in chess has better chances when he plays with the white pieces, but there are times when brilliant games are won with the black pieces.

I will end this section with several quotes from different pages of one of the best chess books I read that teaches beginners by Sunil Weeramantry & Ed Eusebi entitled: *Best Lessons of a Chess Coach* (1993). In this book, the authors are explaining chess positions, and they use comments of general advice. I think that these quotes parallel social emotional skills needed in life.

- <u>Control your own destiny</u>. Do not wait for things to happen to you.

- <u>Anticipate trouble before it happens.</u>

- This means always going one step further in analysis. <u>Learn to push yourself.</u>

Teaching Life Skills Through Chess

- Every move of a chess game is a decision in which you have to balance advantages and disadvantages. One guideline you can use to help make such a decision is: <u>Avoid saddling yourself with a long-term weakness</u>.

- It is very important to come up with a <u>good long-term plan</u>. That's where chess is hard. You must understand that when you play chess you are playing two games. It is you against him, and he against you. You must put yourself in his position and ask "<u>If I were playing his side what would I do</u>?"… when you start making this effort, you will become a much stronger player.

- When he made this move… It is a short-term move. "He is only thinking one move ahead…" the long-term consequences are enormous.

- <u>Think before you move</u>. Identify the position. Examine possible alternatives. Evaluate each alternative.

Directory Of Chess Positions To Be Used In Counseling

The following chess positions are analogous to life situations. There are millions of chess possibilities within each chess game. Each move made by a player changes the situation on the board. Advantages and disadvantages come and go. The outcome of each game rests upon using the forces at your disposal in the most effective way you can. You must adapt and learn from each position. In this chapter, the focus is not to teach chess strategies, but to help students to better cope with their personal situations and decisions. By learning to resolve chess problems, students learn problem-solving strategies that can be used in other situations. Some positions are very simple and only require basic knowledge of how the pieces move. Others are more difficult and require a better understanding of the game.

Directory Of Chess Positions

Several positions have the same pattern. The counselor can become familiar with these situations and stop a game to initiate the conversation. Other times, you can start the session by choosing one of them. It is necessary to adapt the positions to the level of your audience, but it is important to remember that there are chess players as young as 11 who are chess masters. Therefore, some primary students can understand complex positions and gain insight for their own problem-solving situations. The chess positions are organized by topics.

To follow the explanations, we used algebraic notation. The files (rows going up) are lettered a to h. The ranks (rows going across) are numbered 1 to 8. Any square on the board can be identified by combining a letter and a number.

We used this combination of letters and numbers to describe a move from the original position of the piece to the end position. We also used the drawing to identify each piece.

Teaching Life Skills Through Chess

PUZZLE #1

CONFLICT RESOLUTION/FIGHTS

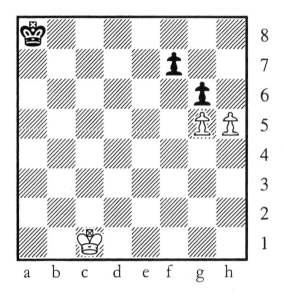

The black pawn just moved forward. It's white's turn to move. **What would you do ?**

    a.- Capture the black pawn (h5-g6)

    b.- Move forward (h5-h6)

Directory Of Chess Positions

The best answer is b.

If the white pawn moves forward, nobody can stop it. It will be promoted to a Queen and later the black King will be checkmated. But if white captures the black pawn, the other black pawn will capture it back and nobody will win. It will be a draw.

ADVICE FOR LIFE

When somebody challenges you, bothers you or steps in your space, your first reaction may be to bother them back or fight. Is this the best decision?

It may be better to think before you move, focus on your goal, and move away from trouble.

Fighting does not resolve anything, nobody wins.

Teaching Life Skills Through Chess

PUZZLE #2

FINDING YOUR OWN SKILLS AND INDIVIDUALITY

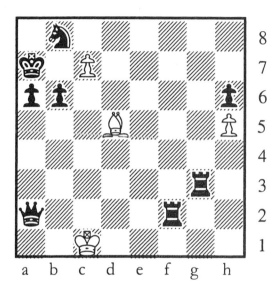

Black player has better pieces on the board. It's white's turn to play. **What would you do?**

a.- Capture the black queen with the bishop. (♗d5 x ♛a2)

b.- Move the white pawn forward and promote to a queen. (c7-c8 = ♕)

c.- Move the white pawn forward and promote to a knight. (c7-c8 = ♘)

The best answer is c.

All the other answers, a, and b will result in black checkmating white. If you choose option a, capturing the queen, the black rook (g2) will move to the end of the file (g3) and checkmate the white king. If you choose b, and the pawn is promoted to a queen, the black rook or queen moves to the end of the file and checkmates the white king. But if you under promote the pawn to a knight (c), the black king is checkmated with the help of the white bishop.

ADVICE FOR LIFE

You must know all your skills and understand their power. In this situation, if you think that promoting to a queen is the best move because the queen is the "most powerful" piece in the game...you are wrong. A knight is better. The knight is less powerful but it moves in a special way (the " L" shape) which can attack over other pieces. You do not need to be "the most powerful" to be successful in the game and in life. If you understand the potential of your own uniqueness and make sound decisions, you will have many opportunities to achieve success in life.

You need to develop all your skills and use them wisely.

Teaching Life Skills Through Chess

PUZZLE #3

STEALING

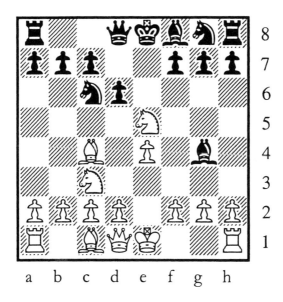

White player just made a "bad move", his knight captures a pawn (e5), but his queen (d1) is in danger. The black bishop can capture it. It's black's turn to move. **What would you do?**

a.- Capture the queen with the bishop (♝g4 x ♕d1)

b.- Capture the knight with the black knight (♞c6 x ♘e5)

Directory Of Chess Positions

The best answer is b.

It is very attractive to capture the queen. But if the black bishop captures the queen it will be a big mistake. The white bishop will capture the black pawn in front of the bishop (f7) and check the king. The black king can only move one space forward in front of him and then is checkmated by the next move from the white knight that moves toward the center of the board (d5).

ADVICE FOR LIFE

A classmate forgets his bag with valuables inside (a CD player)...like the queen. What would you do?... At this particular moment, you do not see anybody, you are not thinking ahead... you only see the opportunity to take something that you like... So you take the CD, (the bishop takes the queen) and this action has terrible consequences. You think that your actions do not have negative consequences..., but white moves his pieces wisely (somebody finds out that you took the CD)... You lose the game, the police become involved, the school suspends you...

> **Think of what could happen as a result of your actions. Look at the long term consequences.**

PUZZLE #4

MAKING WISE DECISIONS

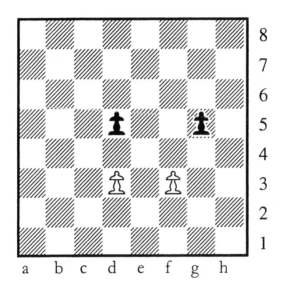

It's black's turn to play. **What would you do?**

a.- Move the d pawn forward. (d5-d4)

b.- Move the g pawn forward. (g5-g4)

The best answer is a.

If you move the "g" pawn, the other player will capture your pawn and win the game. If you move the "d " pawn, the white pawn in the d file is blocked. Then white must move the other pawn (on the f file) allowing the black pawn to capture it. In this scenario, black will win the game.

ADVICE FOR LIFE

In life, you must anticipate trouble before it happens. You must understand the consequences of your actions. You must think before you move. Sometimes, there are simple decisions that appear easy to resolve. In this example of only two pawns that are very near each other, it is easy to see the consequences of your actions.

It is like if you are in the classroom and the teacher asks for your homework, you can anticipate what will happen if you do not turn in it. (Your teacher has stated that not turning in homework results in missing recess). So when you are at home in the afternoon you can do your homework or not. What will you do?

> **Anticipate trouble before it happens.**

Teaching Life Skills Through Chess

PUZZLE #5

GOAL SETTING

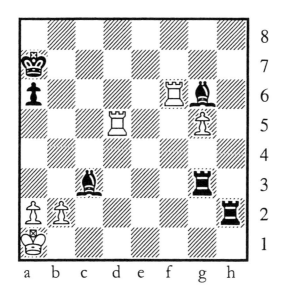

It's white's turn to move. **What would you do?**

a.- Rook to d7 checking the king. (♖ d5 to d7)

b.- Pawn captures the bishop on c3. (♙ b2 x ♝ c3)

c.- Rook to f7. (♖ f6 to f7)

Directory Of Chess Positions

The best answer is a.

Any of the other answers will not checkmate the king, but rook to d7, followed by moving the other rook to f8 does result in a checkmate. With b, the pawn captures the bishop, but then the black rook will move from g3 to g1 and checkmate later the white king. In c, the rook will check the black king, but the bishop on g6 will capture it.

ADVICE FOR LIFE

You must understand your goals in life. In the game of chess, your goal is to checkmate the opponent. You have different goals in each stage of your development in life. In school, one of your goals is to pass a course. You must carefully choose and move in the right direction to achieve that goal. Sometimes, you need to do it step by step. You need to do your homework and study (first check from the rook) and later this will help you to do well on tests in order to pass the course (second move from the rook to checkmate).

> This process of goal setting involves careful planning and thinking ahead.

Teaching Life Skills Through Chess

PUZZLE #6

SHORT TERM GOALS AND LONG TERM GOALS

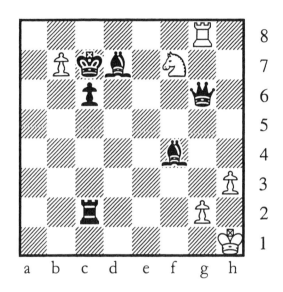

It's white's turn to move. **What would you do?**

a.- Promote the pawn in b7 to a queen. (b7 - b8=♕)

b.- Capture the black queen with the rook.(♖ g8 x ♛ g6)

The best answer is a.

Capturing the queen is a short-term goal. In chess, it is important to understand short-term goals, but it is important to focus on the long-term goal: checkmate. By promoting to a queen you checkmate black. Capturing the queen gets you checkmated by the rook moving to c1.

ADVICE FOR LIFE

There are short term goals and long term goals to achieve. If you understand the objective of the game, you will move "your pieces" in a way that will allow you to win. In chess, sometimes, people are only thinking of capturing pieces without a plan.

When we made this move, capturing the queen, it was a short term move. We were only thinking one move ahead, the long term consequences are enormous (you lose the game). We must understand short term goals and long term goals. If in life, you only focus on getting things or doing things without any long term plan, you will have less opportunities to be successful. For example, drinking, smoking, using illegal drugs, having unprotected sexual relations before you are ready to deal with the consequences.

> **Control your own destiny.**
> **Do not wait for things to happen to you.**

PUZZLE #7

HEALTHY DEVELOPMENT

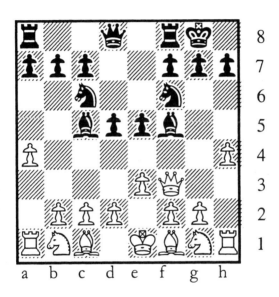

Look at this position. **What player is in a better position?**

    a.- Black

    b.- White

The best answer is a.

Black has developed the pieces in the right way. He has followed the principle of controlling the center and developing pieces and saving the king. The white player has developed the two pawns away from the center. The queen is the only piece that has been developed and moved around a lot. The white king is not castled yet.

ADVICE FOR LIFE

It is very important to develop in a healthy manner. You must eat, exercise regularly and avoid drugs and alcohol. You must learn organization, planning, assertiveness, homework, and study skills to be successful in school.

Sometimes, you have not learned these skills in the primary grades, but you can start any time. Sometimes, in the game of chess although you have not developed your pieces appropriately in the beginning, you can still improve in the middle of the game and in the end be able to win. It is more difficult if you have not started correctly, but it is not impossible to win if you understand the goals and make sound decisions. Therefore, you can learn and try harder to achieve success any time you want to do it.

> **It is very important to develop in a healthy manner.**

Teaching Life Skills Through Chess

PUZZLE #8

TAKING RISKS

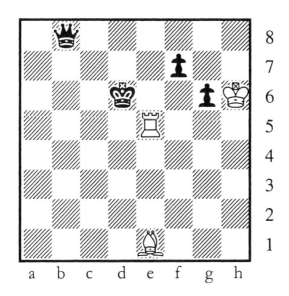

It's black's turn. **What would you do?**

a.- King captures rook on e5. (♚ d6 x ♖ e5)

b.- Queen moves to h8 and checks the king.(♛ b8 - h8 +)

The best answer is b.

Black will take a big risk by capturing the white rook because if white moves the bishop to g3 the black king is in check. The king must move away and later the bishop will capture the black queen. This chess tactic is called a skewer. The black player does not know if the white player will move the bishop to g3. It is a big risk to take the rook that way. It is better to move the queen to h8 and check the black king and attack the rook at the same time. This chess tactic is called a fork.

ADVICE FOR LIFE

Life is full of risks. Sometimes, taking a risk will help you to get something positive. Other times, taking a risk may get you in big trouble. We have to learn to evaluate our situations and evaluate the risks we are facing. How much control do we have to decrease our level of risk?

In the chess position, the black players must count on the possibility that maybe the other player will not see the best move... Are you going to take that risk when somebody suggests that you skip school, try alcohol, drugs, sex, and/or provokes you to fight in school?

> Avoid saddling yourself with a long-term weakness because you took a big risk.

Chapter 4

Chess Counseling Programs

C hess as an Analogy for Life Situations was introduced to counseling students at Lincoln Middle School, Deal Junior High School, Tubman Elementary School and Bell Multicultural High School in 1992. These schools are inner-city schools with a high proportion of minorities and at-risk youth. Students in these schools were introduced to chess as a way to help them better understand their choices and the control they can have over their lives. I created groups that met during recess and after school. Some students participated in chess tournaments.

From 1993-95, I was an elementary school counselor at Bancroft Elementary School in the District of Columbia. This is a K-5 school in the heart of Adams Morgan in the northwest part of the city. The students were principally of African-American and Hispanic descent. About seventy five percent of them were in a free or reduced lunch program. When I implemented my comprehensive counseling program in this school, the use of chess was a big part of it. A teacher evaluation of the success of the chess program showed that more than 80% of the teachers agreed or strongly agreed to the statement: *"Students who have been involved in the chess program have changed in a positive way."*

In the beginning, it was difficult to sell the idea to teachers, but with the support of the Principal of the school, Erasmo Garza, the teachers started accepting the idea. When I conducted guidance classes with chess, some teachers were surprised how well the students from the primary grades learned to play chess. Some students wrote poetry and stories about chess in the school newspaper. A chess club was also established. Students played chess during recess or at lunch and one day after school. During the first meetings of the chess club, few kids came, but by the end of school year the kids were playing chess on the floor of the gym because there was not enough space in the classroom to hold the chess club meeting. We held several chess tournaments at the school. More than 100 students participated in these tournaments. Some students became very good at chess and wanted to play in larger tournaments outside of the school.

The school sent students to the 1995 D. C. Public Schools Championship held at the U.S. Chess Center. The Center is a non-profit organization that focuses on the teaching of chess primarily to disadvantaged students as the vehicle to break out of a cycle of poverty. David Mehler, Executive Director, is most impressed with some of his students

Teaching Life Skills Through Chess

who no longer play chess. Those who are now in college or working at jobs that do not permit them enough time to pursue chess are his greatest successes. Mr. Mehler's leadership helped my chess program to grow. Bancroft students took first place in the Primary Section as well as the Elementary Section. Two students from the school, Giovanni and George took individual first places. Bancroft's students started playing chess during their recess on a big chess set donated by the American Board Association. The students with the help of volunteers painted a big chess board on the playground.

Chess for Success

In the fall of 1996, I started working as an ESOL Bilingual Counselor in the Montgomery County Public Schools in Maryland. Montgomery County is a large system with more than seven thousand ESOL students. I was assigned to serve ESOL students from the Blair Cluster. The Blair Cluster is located in Silver Spring, in the southern part of the county. The cluster has a large high school called Montgomery Blair, three middle schools and eleven elementary schools. The schools have a large minority and low-income population.

Following the model that Montgomery County Public Schools has developed: Success for Every Student, I created and implemented a counseling program called "**Chess For Success**".

Chess Counseling Programs

The Chess for Success program is primarily designed for the ESOL/METS students; ESOL stands for English for Speakers of Other languages and METS stands for Multi-disciplinary Educational Training and Support Program. Students who are in METS had at least two years of interrupted education in their native country.

> **The Chess for Success program links chess strategies to guidance and counseling topics.**

The purpose of this program is to help ESOL students experience success and achievement even when their English proficiency is limited. Instruction in chess and the use of chess in guidance/counseling discussions form a powerful combination for the ESOL student's achievement in schools. It also provided an opportunity for students from different languages, cultures, and backgrounds to interact in a positive social environment.

Description of Student Population

The main target population of the Chess for Success Program is ESOL/METS students attending public elementary, middle and high Schools in Montgomery County's Blair Cluster. Guidance Presentations, Group Counseling, Individual Counseling, and After School Chess Clubs are conducted to address the needs of the students.

ESOL/METS students must overcome the challenges of learning English while maintaining their studies in the content areas. They must understand the process of learning a second language, and during that process feel capable of achieving academic success. They must adjust to a new school and community environment in a positive way that will foster their motivation toward success. They need to understand that the school experience can be exciting and fun and that language is part of intellectual ability, but not all.

They need to think for themselves, foster critical thinking and problem solving skills. Above all, they must understand that success requires patience and perseverance, developing work habits, and making good and informed decisions.

ESOL students are at greater risk of not working at their full potential and dropping out of school, if we don't address their needs. Teachers, administrators, and school based counselors are working toward that goal. The Chess for Success Program added its seeds for success. The program is helping ESOL students to increase their motivation for schoolwork and heighten their sense of responsibility for their own learning. In turn, this is leading to increased participation in the mainstream as they make the transition from ESOL/METS programs to the general school program.

During the first year, four schools were part of the program; in the last year twelve schools have been involved in the program in some form.

Evaluation from teachers

The impact of the Chess for Success Program was evaluated during the group/guidance presentations. At the end of each school year, a questionnaire was presented to the teachers of the students in the program. The teachers were present when I was conducting the sessions. According to the surveys from the teachers, during the last five years of implementing the program all of them (100%) answered positively that they would like for their students to continue their involvement in the Chess For Success program. Specific scores from each question varied, however, the results of the survey and comments reflect the positive impact of the program among students.

These are some of the written comments from teachers.

Ms. Carlson, ESOL teacher, wrote, *"I have seen the students grow as they learned more and listened to them discuss a variety of issues during the sessions. Sometimes, Mr. Moreno was able to raise issues that I had concerns about, but was unable or unsure about how to approach myself. He related behavior to chess and then branched out from there. This gave students something concrete to begin with and also made the discussion non-threatening."*

Ms. Grossman, ESOL teacher, wrote, *"Learning to play chess has helped my ESOL students to see they can be successful at something academic."*

Teaching Life Skills Through Chess

Ms. Holmes, ESOL teacher wrote, *"I have been fortunate enough to have had Mr. Moreno teach counseling with chess to my level 2 ESOL class. I have a bright, eager group who are first beginning to "take off" in English proficiency, and I wanted them to experience success with the thinking and strategy skills they would develop through chess. This class has surpassed my expectations. Students are communicating with students of different languages and cultures; boys are playing girls, outspoken students are paired with shy, quiet students. And through it all, they are learning, thinking, memorizing, acting out their convictions. I see the growth taking place week by week. Chess is an excellent vehicle for growth in interpersonal relations, confidence in self, thinking, and it is helpful for students as they reflect on how their decisions and actions impact on them and others. Finally, chess is a great game that is played around the world. The students are learning a new "Skill for life" and so am I!."*

Ms. Jhen, ESOL teacher, wrote a song with the tune of "My Bonnie Lies Over the Ocean." Her students sang that song at the end of the group sessions. I was so touched that I asked her to write the lyrics out for me.

Chorus:

We do thank you. Oh Mr. Moreno we do thank you. We do thank you. Moreno we'll always thank you!

> 1. You've been our dear friend and our teacher. You've helped us to think and be good. We'll

> *treasure the things you have taught us. And follow our goals as we should.*
>
> 2. *We've learned to play chess so completely. We've learned how to win and to lose. And to accept consequences. For all of the things that we choose.*
>
> 3. *And when we play chess we'll remember. Life's decisions are false and true. And we'll live our life with good choices. As our chess mentor taught us to do!*

The next table tabulates the specific responses from teachers. These data are consistent over the 1996 to 2000 years. This book is written in part to help other counselors and other professionals to use this model with their ESOL population. However, I strongly believe that it will work with any school population. Also, in the last two years many classroom teachers requested guidance sessions with their students at their homeroom. I conducted classroom guidance using the game of chess with all their students in the room. I conducted guidance to kindergarten, first and fourth grade classes which included ESOL, Special Education, and Gifted and Talented students.

This year I conducted a Chess For Success Guidance Program at Oak View Elementary School in Silver Spring, Maryland. I conducted it with a whole class, including ESOL and mainstream students. The teacher's comments were very positive.

Teaching Life Skills Through Chess

Ms. White, a fourth grade teacher wrote, *"It engages their attention from start to finish. They learned how to work cooperatively with one another. They learned many skills by participating in the program. All of them, ESOL and mainstream students learned. It teaches how to think before they act. It teaches different strategies to use to solve problems"*

Teacher Evaluation Table

Questions (% agree/ strongly agree)	Year 1996	Year 1997	Year 1998	Year 1999	Year 2000
I would like my ESOL/METS students to continue their involvement in the chess program.	100%	100%	100%	100%	100%
Through the game of chess ESOL/METS students have increased their social skills	100%	96%	96%	98%	96%
Learning to play chess has helped ESOL/ METS students to increase their awareness of their strengths and weakness.	72%	72%	74%	72%	76%
Learning to play chess has helped ESOL/METS students to better understand the decision making process.	86%	80%	84%	86%	90%

Chess Counseling Programs

Questions (% agree/ strongly agree)	Year 1996	Year 1997	Year 1998	Year 1999	Year 2000
Learning to play chess has helped ESOL/ METS students to better understand and cope with their frustration level. (learning in a new environment/ language, etc.)	86%	90%	90%	86%	90%
Learning to play chess has helped ESOL/ METS students to better evaluate their decisions and predict positive or negative consequences of their actions	86%	86%	88%	90%	86%
Learning to play chess is a good tool to help ESOL/METS students focus more on school work	72%	74%	72%	76%	80%
ESOL/METS students who participate in the chess program have shown progress in a positive way	72%	76%	80%	80%	84%

The teacher evaluations for individual student counseling sessions to analyze the strength of chess as a counseling model were very difficult to produce. The principal reason is because I did not use only "chess" to counsel students. However, I have anecdotal data to confirm that my individual counseling sessions have been effective. For example, one ESOL teacher, Ms. Barkley, wrote to me, *"He has started to turn in more reading homework. He stays in at recess to finish his projects and unfinished homework."*

Teachers, parents and administrators have informed me that the students I work with have changed in a positive way. Also, they have sent comments to my supervisor requesting the continuation of my assignment to their schools. This could be easily interpreted as confirmation that my counseling program, with the use of chess as part of it, is working successfully.

Evaluation from students

The ESOL//METS students who participated in the group and/or guidance sessions evaluated the Chess for Success Program. Many of them did not know how to play chess prior to this program. Almost all of them learned the basic rules of the game and played games against other students. Some participated in chess tournaments and won trophies and medals.

One of the most important conclusions of the student data is that they like learning and playing chess. Almost all of the students responded positively to chess. But only approximately 70% of students want to participate in a chess club. This shows that chess should not be exclusively an after-school activity. Students like to play and learn from chess, in the context of classroom guidance but many will not participate as much in a chess club.

These are some of the students' comments;

" Chess is fun and helps people."

"Chess has helped me to learn to make decisions."

"Chess has helped me to understand things and choices."

"Chess helped me to see that I can do things."

"Chess has helped me to respect other students."

"Chess helped me to think more."

"Chess is fun and when I go with friends, we play chess and have fun."

"Chess makes me think about things that I should not do and what happens if I do it."

"Chess helped me to see the consequences of my behavior."

"Chess is like life, you move and the other player moves, you must be aware of dangers and think to avoid problems."

Teaching Life Skills Through Chess

Student Evaluation Table

Questions (% of Yes answers)	Year 1996	Year 1997	Year 1998	Year 1999	Year 2000
Have you liked learning about chess?	98%	96%	98%	97%	98%
I would like to continue playing chess?	95%	93%	94%	96%	96%
I would recommend learning to play chess to other ESOL students.	80%	78%	85%	80%	85%
Would you like to create a chess club?	68%	69%	74%	74%	69%

From all of these evaluations, I concluded that the use of chess as an analogy of life situations and a model in school counseling had positive outcomes with the ESOL population in Montgomery County Public Schools.

It can prove successful with any student population if it is adapted to their needs. Over and above, the use of chess to teach life skills to youth is easy and designed to succeed.

Chess Counseling Programs

Several counselors in MCPS and around the country are asking me about this approach. I have been asked to present at several conferences, the last one was the 2001 Best Practices Seminar Conference for school counselors organized for Montgomery County Public School in Rockville, Maryland this past Spring.

As a final note, I strongly believe that this approach has many possibilities, and I encourage people who work in the field to try it and develop it with their own creativity to help children and adolescents to find the best path in their lives.

Teaching Life Skills Through Chess

Resources About Chess

To find information about any instructional materials in the US and/or buy chess equipment:

U.S. Chess Federation
Tom Brownscombe, Scholastic Director
3054 US Rte 9W
New Windsor, NY 12553
Phone: 1-845-562-8350
Web- page: www.uschess.org

U.S. Chess Center
David Mehler, Director
1501 M Street, NW
Washington, DC 20005
Phone (202) 857-4922
web-page: www.chessctr.org

For information in training how to use chess in guidance and counseling

Fernando Moreno
8004 Carroll Ave.
Takoma Park, Maryland 20912
Phone:(301) 431-0062
E-mail: Morenofe@AOL.com

References

"Chess For Success" (1997, January).*NEA today*, pp. 14. Washington,DC

Coker K.(2001) Creative Arts in Counseling with Elementary School Children. Elementary School Counseling in the New Millennium. Alexandria, VA: American Counseling Association

Steiern, G. (1993). The Royal Knight of Harlem. *Chicken Soup for the Soul, 101 Stories to Open the Heart and Rekindle the Spirit.* Deerfield Beach, Florida: Health Communication, Inc.

"ESOL Chess project wins national award" (October 14,1996). *The Bulletin, pp.1-3* . Montgomery County Public Schools.

Ferguson, R. (1995). "Chess in education summary" (USCF chess in Education 1995 Annual Conference) New Windsor: United States Chess Federation.

Garden R.A.(1988). The Game of Checkers in Child Therapy. *Game Play*. New York : John Wiley & Sons.

Goleman, D.(1995). *Emotional Intelligence: Why it can matter more than IQ*. New York: Battman Book.

Guerra P. (1998, July). Counseling Program uses chess as an analogy for life situations. *Counseling Today,* pp. 44-45.

References

Hawkins D.(1992). W.T. Grant Consortium on the School-Based Promotion of Social Competence. *Communities Than Care.* San Francisco: Jossey-Bass.

Horgan D. (1987). Chess as a Way to teach Thinking. Paper. New Windsor: United States Chess Federation.

Leff, L (1993). Maneuvering to Win Young Minds. Playing The Game, Mastering Their Lives. *Washington Post.* May17,1993.

Moreno, F. (1999, Spring). Chess among school counselors. *Chess Coach Newsletter.* New Windsor: United States Chess Federation.

Oklander, V. (1988). *Windows* to our children. Highland, NY: The Gestalt Journal Press.

Palm, C.(1990) Chess Improves Academic Performance. Paper. *New York City Schools Chess Program.*

Schaefer C. & Reid S. (1988). The Psychology of Play in Games. *Game Play.* New York : John Wiley & Sons.

Weeramantry, S & Eusebi E. (1993). *Best Lessons of a Chess Coach.* New York: Mckay Chess Library.

About the Author

Fernando Moreno, is a Psychologist trained in Spain and holds a Master's degree in School Counseling from Trinity College, Washington, D. C. Mr. Moreno has attained certification as a National Certified Counselor (NCC) and works as a Bilingual/ESOL School Counselor in Montgomery County Public Schools, Maryland. Mr. Moreno has been working with (K-12) students and their families from different countries and backgrounds for more than 12 years in the U.S.

He has presented his work in different conferences in and out of the U.S. His latest presentation was at Montgomery College in the Best Practices Fair for Counselors in MCPS on May 24, 2001. He has also presented his work at the 2000 World Conference of the American Counseling Association celebrated in Washington, DC on March 21, 2000. He presented at the University of Maryland, Baltimore Campus in the "Chess in Education Symposium" held on April 16, 1999.

Mr. Moreno's work has been featured in many articles in local newspapers. The latest one appeared in the *Gazette* (4/14/99). *NEA Today* featured Mr. Moreno's work in their "Innovators Section" (January 1997). *Counseling Today* featured an article about Mr. Moreno's work (July, 1998). Mr. Moreno received national recognition because of his innovative use of chess. The USCF commended his initiative in employing chess strategies to teach real life lessons. The ceremony was held at the U.S. Capitol on September 17, 1996.